Jan Thompson

Foundation

Hodder & Stoughton
A MEMBER OF THE HODDER HEADLINE GROUP

Dedicated to:
Joyce Mackley, a friend and colleague.

The author wishes to thank the following for their generous help with this book: Canon Ian Dunlop; The Reverend David Bowers; Bishop Allison; The Reverend Huw Mosford; Peter Cotterell; Melvyn Fancy; the parents of Andrea Jackson; Marise, Mark, Rosalind and Sally; Sandy, Lynne and Alison; The Reverend Ros Parrett.

Notes:

> CE = Common Era.
> BCE = Before the Common Era.
>
> CE corresponds to AD, and BCE corresponds to BC. The years are the same, but CE and BCE can be used by anyone regardless of their religion. (AD and BC are Christian: AD stands for Anno Domini – in the Year of Our Lord, i.e. Jesus Christ; BC stands for Before Christ.)

Key words are explained in the Glossary on page 63

Order queries: please contact Bookpoint Ltd, 39 Milton Park, Abingdon, Oxon OX14 4TD. Telephone: (44) 01235 400414, Fax: (44) 01235 400454. Lines are open from 9.00–6.00, Monday to Saturday, with a 24 hour message answering service. Email address: orders@bookpoint.co.uk

British Library Cataloguing in Publication Data
A catalogue record for this title is available from The British Library

ISBN 0 340 77580 7

First published 2000
Impression number   10 9 8 7 6 5 4 3 2 1
Year   2004 2003 2002 2001 2000

Cover photo from Christine Osborne Pictures/MEP.
All illuastrations supplied by Daedalus, with special thanks to John McIntyre
Typeset by Wearset, Boldon, Tyne and Wear.
Printed for Hodder & Stoughton Educational, a division of Hodder Headline Plc, 338 Euston Road, London NW1 3BH by Printer Trento, Italy.

The Publishers would like to thank the following for permission to reproduce copyright photographs in this book: AKG, London: pp5, 6, 16, 48r; Mark Azavedo: p56r; Bureau Medicale de Notre Dame de Lourdes: p53; Christian Aid: p62l (Adrian Arbib), 62r (Leah Gordon); CIRCA Photo Library: pp14 (Martin Palmer) 20, 35b (Bipin J Mistry), 46l (John Fryer), 60; Corbis: pp41, 56l, 57; Philip Emmett: pp9br, 15, 21tr, 42, 47r, 52; Courtesy of Dawn French and Sue Hunter: p39; Melanie Friend/Format: p36; Sally Lancaster/Format: p61; Life File: pp34 (Emma Lee), 40 (Wayne Shakell), 43 (Sergei Verein), 51l (Mike Evans), 54 (Graham Burns); Network Photographers: p9tr; Christine Osborne/MEP: pp9l, 18 (G Bonatt), 21bl, 35t, 55; Hans Reinhard/OKAPIA/OSF: p17; Marcus Perkins: p27; David Rose: pp7, 10, 21tl, 22, 23, 46r, 47l, 48l, 49l, 50; Still Pictures/Bojan Brecelj: p19; Jan Thompson: p32b; Topham Picturepoint: p17; Alan Watson/Forest Light: p49r.

The Publishers would like to thank the following for permission to reproduce material in this volume: The Archbishops' Council of the Church of England for The Apostles' Creed from *The Alternative Service Book 1980*, copyright © The Archbishops' Council of the Church of England and reproduced by permission; BBC TV for the extract from *England's Nazareth*; Christian Aid for the extract from *Christian Aid News*, April/June 1999; Peter Cotterell for the extract from *This is Christianity* (1985); Hugs illustration reprinted from *The Second Tiny Book of Hugs* by Kathleen Keating and Mimi Noland, published by HarperCollins Publishers. Copyright © 1988 by Kathleen Keating, drawings by Mimi Noland. All rights reserved. Reproduced by permission of Multimedia Product Development, Chicago, Illinois; Salvationist Publishing and Supplies Ltd for the extract from their publicity leaflet; The United Society for the Propagation of the Gospel for the extract from *USPG Network*; World Council of Churches for the Oikoumene logo.

Minor adaptations have been made to some quotations to render them more accessible to the readership.

Every effort has been made to contact the holders of copyright material but if any have been inadvertently overlooked, the publisher will be pleased to make the necessary alterations at the first opportunity.

Contents

Jesus

The Christian religion is called Christianity. It is named after Jesus Christ. He was a Jew who lived 2,000 years ago. He lived in the country now called Israel.

TASK

- Talk about anything you already know about Jesus.
- Can you remember any Bible stories about him?

Jesus was a teacher and healer. He was popular with the people. But the Jews' leaders were afraid of him. They complained to the Romans, who were in charge. Jesus was hanged on a cross and killed. This is called the Crucifixion.

▼ Artists all over the world have painted pictures of Jesus. This one of Jesus and his mother, Mary, is from India

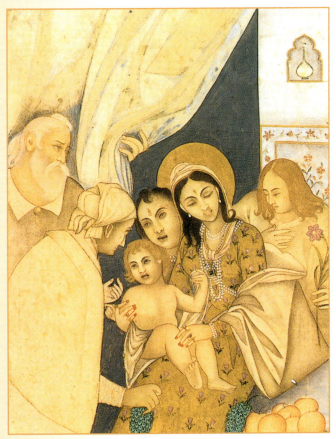

Look at the map below. Can you find these places?

- Bethlehem – where Jesus was born
- Galilee – where Jesus lived and worked
- Jerusalem – where Jesus died.

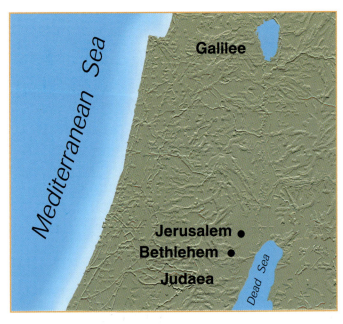

▲ Where Christianity started

▲ *Jesus heals a blind man*

There are many stories about Jesus healing people. This story names the 4 most important disciples. (Simon was also called Peter.) It also tells us why Jesus believed he was sent.

Jesus went with James and John to the home of Simon and Andrew. Simon's mother-in-law was in bed with a fever. Jesus went to her, took her hand and helped her up. The fever left her and she was well enough to look after them.

Many sick people were taken to Jesus. The whole town turned out! There were crowds at the door. Jesus healed many of them.

Jesus got up very early the next morning while it was still dark. He left the house and went off to be alone to pray.

Simon and the others came looking for him. When they found him, they said, 'Everybody is looking for you.' Jesus said, 'Let's go somewhere else, so that I can teach. For that is why I came.'

Retold from Mark chapter 1 verses 29–38

Jesus was killed. But that was not the end of the story. Christians believe that God brought Jesus back to life. This is called the Resurrection. They believe that Jesus was seen by his followers before he went back to heaven.

Jesus had many followers. The main ones were his 12 disciples. They carried on Jesus' work. They started the Christian Church.

Why was Jesus sent?

Christians believe that Jesus was sent to show people what God is like. 'Christ' wasn't his name. It was a special title. It meant that he was filled with God's Spirit. He could speak for God.

Key words

Jesus Christ	Crucifixion
Resurrection	heaven
disciples	

1 With your partner, read the words in the word-box. Make sure you know what they mean. You can look them up in the glossary at the back of this book.

2 Write down FOUR things about Jesus' life. Which do you think a Christian would say is most important? Talk about it with a partner.

3 Why do Christians think that Jesus was sent? What answer does Jesus give at the end of the story above?

Christians believe that God sent Jesus to be their Saviour – to save them from their sins (the wrong things they do).

Christians believe that Jesus is the Son of God – that he shows people what God is like. Jesus taught people to love God and to love each other. Christians believe that he helps them to live as God wants.

A Christian woman explains what Jesus means to her:

> He is a life-saver and a friend. He is someone I can talk to and share my thoughts and feelings with. This is often a great help just to sort things out in my mind.
>
> I think of Jesus as wise, good and kind. When I ask him, he helps me to see what I ought to do. He speaks to me through my conscience. He lets me know when I have done something wrong.
>
> Jesus died on the cross to pay for the sins of the world. When I sin, I cause him pain. You wouldn't want to cause pain to a friend. So I don't want to cause pain to Jesus.

▲ *Jesus goes up to heaven*

Key words

sin
conscience

1 The woman above has used the words 'sin' and 'conscience'. Write a sentence for each of these words. Show that you understand what they mean. (You can look them up in the glossary.)

2 How does the woman talk to Jesus? How does she think he answers her?

3 The woman thinks of Jesus as her friend.
  a) List FIVE things Jesus does (or has done) for her.
  b) What does she do for Jesus?

4 a) Why doesn't she want to hurt Jesus?
  b) Think of a time when you hurt a friend. How did you feel?

The new Christian religion grew fast. In AD 325 it became the religion of the Roman Empire. It spread to different countries, with different leaders of the Church.

In 1054 the Churches in the East split from those in the West. They argued about who should be the main leader of the Church. The Eastern Orthodox Churches had their centre in Constantinople (now called Istanbul, in Turkey). The Western Church had its centre in Rome, in Italy. Christians in the West became known as Roman Catholics. Their leader was the Bishop of Rome, also called the Pope. About half the Christians in the world today are Roman Catholics.

About 500 years later the Roman Catholic Church split again. Some Christians protested at the way it was run. New Churches were set up. They were called Protestant Churches, because of their protests.

The Church of England also broke away from the Roman Catholic Church in 1534. But it was a mix of old and new, Catholic and Protestant. Another name for the Church of England is Anglican.

Since then, many other Christian Churches have started. Today there are millions of Christians around the world. It is the biggest religion in the world.

▲ *Archbishop Gregorias is a leader of the Eastern Orthodox Church*

7

Key words

Eastern Orthodox	Roman Catholic
Protestant	Anglican

1 Find out the name of the present Pope.

◄ *The Christian family and some of its many branches*

▼ *Badge of the World Council of Churches. (OIKOUMENE means the whole world.)*

There are many different brands of washing powder.   But they all do the same thing.   They have different names and colours.   They come in different packets.   But they all wash clothes.   In the same way, **there are many different styles of Christianity, but they are all the same religion**.   They all believe in God and Jesus.

The different Churches are now trying to come together again.   They talk to each other.   They try to understand their differences.   Some Churches work and worship together whenever they can.

Many different Churches now belong to the World Council of Churches.   You can see its badge in the picture.   There is a cross in a boat on the sea.   This is because all Christians are 'in the same boat' in the world.

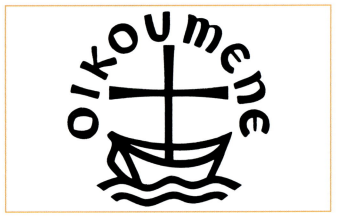

1 Look at the diagram of the Church as a tree. Write out this list of Churches in the order in which they were formed:
Methodist, Anglican, Roman Catholic, Salvation Army, Baptist.

2 a) Copy out the badge of the World Council of Churches.   Write a sentence to explain what it means.

b) Design your own badge for a united Church.   Explain what it means.

Think about any family. People have different interests. They like different music. They want to watch different TV programmes. But there is a family bond.

It is the same with the Christian family. People have different ways of worshipping God. Some like plain churches, others like colourful churches with statues and candles. Some like peace and quiet, others like to sing to brass bands. Some like the old ways, others like the new.

▲ *Worship in an African church*

▲ *Worship in an Armenian Orthadox church*

▲ *Worship in a Protestant church*

1 Work in 3 groups, each with a different photo (above):
   a) Describe in detail what you can see in your photo so that someone who could not see it would be able to imagine what it looks like.
   b) Suggest how the people in your photo feel.

TASK

When you need guidance and advice, where do you go to get it?

The Christian holy book is called the Bible. The Bible looks like one book. But inside its covers there are at least 66 different books, printed on extra-thin paper. They were written by different people at different times. So the Bible is more like a library of books.

There are 2 main parts to the Christian Bible:

1 The Old Testament
2 The New Testament.

Roman Catholics have a third part:

3 The Apocrypha. (The books in the Apocrypha were written between the times of the Old Testament and New Testament.) The Old Testament is also the Jewish Bible.

Jesus was a Jew, and this is the Bible that he would have known. It has 39 different books in it. There are stories and the history of the Jews. There are laws for them to follow. There are poems and wise sayings.

The New Testament was written after Jesus had died. It has 27 books. There are 4 accounts of his life. There are stories about the early Church and letters from the early Church leaders.

The 4 books about Jesus are called Gospels – the Gospels of Matthew, Mark, Luke and John. The word 'gospel' means 'good news'. They are the most important part of the Bible for Christians. They tell the good news about Jesus.

▲ *The Bible is read in church. The Gospel reading, which you can see here, is the most important reading*

1 Using pages 10–11, find THREE reasons why the Bible is important to Christians.

2 One verse in the Bible says, 'Your Word is a lamp for my feet.' In small groups, think about and explain what the writer meant. Draw a poster to illustrate what he meant.

There are millions of books in the world. But Christians choose the Bible to guide them through life. It is like a 'Highway Code' for living.

▲ *We need to find our way on the roads. How do we find our way in life?*

Some Christians read the Bible every day. Many use Bible notes to help them. These take a small part of the Bible each day and explain what it means. They usually end with a prayer. It gives people something to think about during the day.

Some Christians believe that every word of the Bible is true:

> The Bible is the Word of God. He inspired the writers to tell us the truth ... So I believe what the Bible tells me. God would not lie to me. When I read it, I know He is telling me the truth.

Other Christians believe that most things in the Bible come from God. But they say that it was written by ordinary people who could make mistakes:

> They didn't have tape-recorders in those days. It was only at a later stage that they thought, 'We must get this down' ... I don't think we can always say we've got the exact words of Jesus. We've got what was remembered and there could have been small mistakes.

Some Christians underline verses of the Bible that are special to them. Here are some well-known verses:

> I am the way, the truth and the life.
>
> *(Jesus)*
>
> You have heard that it was said, 'You shall love your neighbour and hate your enemy.' But I say to you, 'Love your enemies and pray for those who hate you.'
>
> *(Jesus)*

Key words

Bible	**Apocrypha**
New Testament	**Gospels**
Old Testament	**inspired**

◀ *Jesus heals a blind man*

There are some beautiful verses in the Bible, but there are many things that are very difficult to understand.

There are stories about cruel things done in the name of God. This is usually in the early stories of the Old Testament. People are put to death. Sometimes whole families and tribes are wiped out because they are enemies of the Jews.

Christians point out that these things happened thousands of years ago. As time went by, people came to understand that God was loving and forgiving. Some Christians think that God was slowly teaching his people the right way to live, and what he was really like. By the time of Jesus, people could understand that God was love. They could understand that those who worshipped this God must be loving too. They must forgive their enemies. 2000 years later, and we still find this difficult to do!

Another difficulty for some Christians is how to understand the miracles in the Bible. Did they really happen? Did Jesus really heal people? And the biggest miracle of all – did the Resurrection really take place?

Christians have different views on this. Some believe them exactly as the Bible says. They argue that God who made the world can do anything. Others may look for explanations.

1 Write to some famous people and ask them if they have any favourite verses from the Bible. You could muddle up pictures of the people and their replies. Pupils looking at the display will have to guess who said what.

The Bible says that Adam and Eve were the first man and woman. Some Christians think that stories like this did not really happen. They believe they are special stories to teach people how God wants them to live. So they contain important ideas, even if the stories are made up.

▲ *Adam and Eve know what is right, but they are tempted to do wrong. Today, we still struggle with our conscience*

Some Christians think that the miracle stories were based on real events. Take the 'Feeding of the 5000', for example. The people saw that Jesus was prepared to share his few loaves and fishes. So they may have started to share what they had. The miracle was that Jesus stopped people being selfish.

▲ *Jesus shared the little he had. Perhaps this got everyone else to share their food*

1 The Gideons give free Bibles to **(a)** schools **(b)** hospitals **(c)** hotels **(d)** prisons.
In groups of 4, talk about why you think they do this. A different pupil is to take the lead on **(a)**, **(b)**, **(c)** and **(d)**.

Christian beliefs are summed up in their **creeds**. This word comes from Latin and means 'I believe'. So a creed is a list of Christian beliefs. They are often said as part of a church service.

Here are some of the main points of the Christian creeds:

> - God the Father made heaven and earth.
>
> - Jesus Christ was God's Son.
>
> - Jesus Christ was born the son of the Virgin Mary.
>
> - Jesus Christ was crucified, he died and was buried.
>
> - Jesus Christ rose from the dead after 3 days.
>
> - Jesus Christ went up to heaven.
>
> - Jesus Christ will come again to judge the living and the dead.
>
> - The Holy Spirit is the giver of life.

Christians believe in 1 God, but they call him by 3 different names:

1 God the Father
2 God the Son (Jesus Christ)
3 God the Holy Spirit.

This idea is called the Trinity. It means '3-in-1'. Christians use lots of ways to try to explain this belief. Here are some of them:

- Think of yourself. If you are a boy, you might be a son, a brother and a friend. You are each of these, but you are still one and the same person.

- Think of H_2O. It can be water, steam or ice, but it is still H_2O.

▲ *This shows God the Father (on the right), God the Son (holding a cross), and God the Holy Spirit (as a white, gentle dove)*

▲ *How is God like the sea?   Read the stories on this page*

The Trinity helps Christians to think of God in different ways:

- When Christians think of God the Father, they think of a loving God who looks after his children.   They also think of a powerful God who made the world.
- They think of God the Son as Jesus Christ.   They remember that he died on the cross to save them from their sins.   So they think of God as loving and forgiving.
- Christians think of the Holy Spirit as God inside them, helping them to do right.

Christians know that they can never fully understand God.   He is like a deep ocean. They can only splash around in the shallows.

Talk about these 2 stories with your teacher.   What do they say about God?

Two friends walked by the sea one day and saw a small child running to and from with a bucket, trying to fill a hole in the sand.   The child said, 'I'm trying to put the whole sea into my hole!' The friends smiled and walked on.   How are we like the little child when we think about God?

A fish went around searching for the ocean.   It travelled far and wide, looking here and there. It came to an older fish, and asked, 'Where is the thing called ocean?'   'It is all around you and within you!' answered the older fish.

1 Put the title 'The Trinity'.   Explain this by copying out the 5 lines on page 14, beginning 'Christians believe in one God ...'

2 You have been asked to design an altar cloth for Holy Trinity Church, London. Draw your design, using some of the ideas on the Trinity on pages 14–15. Then write a short letter to the vicar, explaining what your design means.

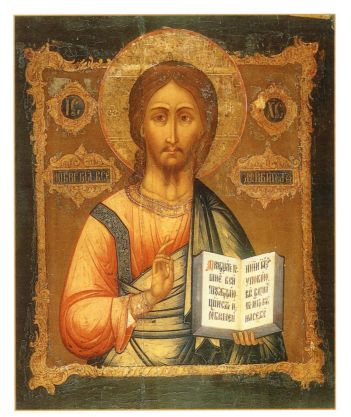

▲ *This is a very old picture of Jesus, but his face is clear. His hand is raised to bless people*

I believe in Jesus Christ, his only Son, our Lord ...

The middle part of the Creed is all about the Son, Jesus Christ. It tells how he was born and how he died. It says that he rose again. (This is called the Resurrection.) It says that he returned to heaven. (This is called the Ascension.)

It also says that Jesus Christ will come again to judge the living and the dead. Christians have different ideas about this. But they all agree that Jesus has not yet finished with the world. They believe that good will win over evil.

> When the Son of Man comes as King ... he will sit on his royal throne, and everybody will be gathered before him. Then he will divide them into 2 groups, just as a shepherd separates the sheep from the goats. He will put the [good] people on his right and the others on his left.
>
> *Matthew chapter 25 verses 31–33*

I believe in the forgiveness of sins ...

We all make mistakes. We do things which we know are wrong. We hurt other people. Christians call this sin. Sin is going against God's wishes. Christians believe that God offers them forgiveness. They must really be sorry for what they have done, and must try not to do it again.

When Jesus died on the cross, he forgave his enemies. Christians see this as the best example of God's love in action. It teaches them that God wants to forgive the sins of the whole world. Christians believe that, on the cross, Jesus took the punishment for the sins of the world. A hymn which Christians sing says this:

> There was no other good enough
> To pay the price of sin;
> He only could unlock the gate
> Of heaven and let us in.

Key words

creed	Ascension
Trinity	hymn
Holy Spirit	

I believe in the Holy Spirit ...

Christians believe that the Holy Spirit is God living around us and in us. They can't see the Holy Spirit, but they know that he is there. In the same way, we can't see the air, but we know it is there because we breathe it! Christians have many symbols for the Holy Spirit. Here are some examples:

▼ *The Holy Spirit is like water. Both give life*

Other symbols for the Holy Spirit:
- wind – because you can't see it, but you can see what it does
- dove – because it is pure and peaceful
- fire – because it is powerful.

The Bible calls the Holy Spirit the Comforter. The word 'comfort' may sound like a soft word – we talk of comfortable armchairs! But it actually means 'give strength'. This is how one Christian explains the idea of God the Holy Spirit as a Comforter:

> Something very painful happened to me when I was a soldier in the war. I broke my leg very badly. A person came and knelt beside me. It was the sergeant-major himself. He actually held my hand!
>
> People were taking my boot off. That was the really painful moment. I could feel from the pressure of his hand in mine, that my pain was becoming his pain. That gave me strength. That is what 'comforter' means. It means to 'strengthen'.
>
> The Holy Spirit is like that. He can give us God's strength.

1 Talk with a friend about a time when you needed comforting. (Remember that the word means that someone gave you strength when you needed it.)

2 Look back over this page to check what Christians mean by God the Holy Spirit. Draw TWO things to stand for the Holy Spirit and explain what they mean.

3 In groups, take a large sheet of paper and draw a cross in the centre. Cut out headlines from newspapers about cruel and sinful events. Stick these around the cross. Underneath, write 'Christians believe that the world needs God's forgiveness.'

▶ *Sunrise follows sunset and the blackness of night. Christians believe new life will follow the darkness of death*

... and the life everlasting

Christians believe that there is a life after death. They believe that we will meet our friends and family again.

But they do not think life after death will be the same as life on earth. It is a different state of existence. Life beyond this world follows different rules. It is beyond time and space.

Christians do not believe that heaven is up above us. The stars and planets are above us. They believe that heaven is like the different levels of a computer game.

▲ *Time to move on to another level*

God himself will be with them ...
He will wipe every tear from their eyes.
There will be no more death
... or crying or pain,
for the old order of things has passed away.

Revelation 21 verses 3–4

This passage from the Bible gives Christians hope in the face of death. When a loved one dies, Christians hold a funeral service. They give thanks for the life of the dead person, and ask God to take care of him or her. It is a time to be sad and to cry for the person they have lost. But Christian funerals also have a note of joy. Christians believe that death is not the end.

TASK

Think and talk about these questions:
- When did you first know about death?
- Why don't people like to talk about death?
- Why might it be helpful to talk about death before someone close to you dies?

British people don't like to show their feelings in public. This has nothing to do with being Christian. Christian funerals can be very different in other parts of the world. Afro-Caribbean funerals, for example, often have an open coffin. People walk past to pay their last respects. They will weep, blow kisses and touch the body. They believe that letting out such feelings is important. It helps people to get over their sadness.

The following prayer is said by the priest at an Anglican funeral. This comes near the end of the service as the body is taken away in the coffin, to be cremated or buried. Notice that the Christian belief in life after death is linked with belief in the Resurrection of Jesus Christ.

> Heavenly Father ... in your love you have given us new life in Christ Jesus. We give this person to your merciful keeping, in the faith of Jesus Christ your Son our Lord, who died and rose again to save us, and is now alive and reigns with you and the Holy Spirit in glory for ever.

1 a) Share ideas about what you think heaven might be like, if it exists. Go round the class, and each finish the sentence 'Heaven is ...'
b) What do Christians think about heaven?

2 a) Collect some obituary notices from a local paper. These announce someone's death and tell you about that person. What phrases do people tend to use?
b) How would you like to be remembered?

3 Make up a children's story about a caterpillar who turns into a chrysalis and then into a butterfly! Tell the story in such a way that it gives the Christian message that death is a change of state, but not to be feared.

Key words

funeral
priest
cremate

19

◀ *A baby is baptised*

> **TASK**
> - In groups, write down all the things water can be used for.
> - Then make a list of words to describe water, like 'refreshing'.

Water is so important that it is used as a symbol. It is a symbol of:
- being made clean inside – this is because it is used for washing.
- death – because people drown in water.
- life – because all living things need water.

Christian baptism is the ceremony when a person joins the Church.   Water is used in this ceremony.   It is used as a symbol to mean that:
- the person has been washed clean of their sins;
- they have died to their old ways;
- they have been given a new Christian life.

Most Churches baptise babies.   Water is usually poured over their heads 3 times.   In Orthodox Churches, the baby is undressed and dipped into the water 3 times.   It is done 3 times in the name of God the Father, Son and Holy Spirit.

The water is in a large basin which is called a font.   (This is like the word 'fount', or 'fountain'.)   You may see a font just inside the door of a church.   This is to show that baptism is the 'doorway' into Christianity.

A baby cannot speak for itself.   So its parents decide to bring the baby for baptism. They promise to bring up the child as a Christian.   This is why some people call it 'Christening'.   The parents choose godparents to help them with this.   The child is called by its name at baptism.   This is why first names used to be called Christian names.

A lighted candle is given. Anglican priests say, 'This is to show that you have passed from darkness to light. Shine as a light in the world.'

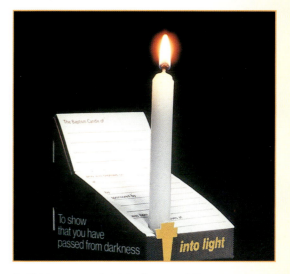

▲ 'Shine as a light in the world'

▲ The priest holds the Gospel over the child's head and prays for her

As well as the water, other special things take place at a baptism. The priest prays that the child will be kept safe from evil. The sign of the cross is made on the child's forehead. This may be done with the water of baptism. Or it may be done with oil that has been blessed. Oil is like God's Holy Spirit – soothing and healing.

► The moment of baptism when the water is poured

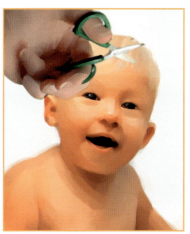

▲ Another custom in some Orthodox churches is that 3 pieces of hair are cut from the child's head. This shows that the child is given to God

▲ 'I sign you with the sign of the cross'

The Baptist Church does not baptise babies. People have to be old enough to believe in Jesus Christ for themselves. So they call it believer's baptism. A Baptist describes what happened to her:

You're baptised in front of everybody. It's your public witness that you want to follow Jesus. The usual way is for a minister to hold your back and your hand. Then, you go backwards into the water. Your feet actually come off the ground. My father, who baptises people, says the problem is getting you under the water because you float!

But the person who baptised me had had polio as a teenager. He hadn't got the strength in his arms to be able to baptise in that way. So I was baptised kneeling down and then I went forward under the water. So there was no fear.

Afterwards, an elderly lady said to me, 'I expect you feel good now.' And I remember being a bit embarrassed and saying, 'I feel clean.' It sounded a silly thing to say. But I just felt totally clean – as if everything had been wiped out. That cleanness right inside was a splendid feeling.

▲ *A believer's baptism in a Baptist Church*

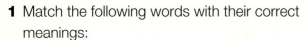

1 Match the following words with their correct meanings:

font	person responsible for the child's religious upbringing
baptism	basin holding water for baptism
godparent	ceremony when a person joins the Church

2 a) Draw a candle. Beneath it, write out the words that the priest says when he or she gives the candle.

b) Talk about what it means for a person to 'shine as a light in the world'.

3 Imagine that you are a vicar in an Anglican church. You want to produce an information sheet for parents who want their baby baptised:

● Write a starting paragraph about what baptism is.

● Under these headings, 'The water', 'The sign of the cross', and 'The candle', describe what will happen to their child and what it means. Illustrate your sheet with pictures.

Babies cannot speak for themselves. That is why parents and godparents make promises for them at baptism. But the time comes when young people must choose for themselves. Do they want to be a Christian or not?

Young members of the Church of England and Roman Catholic Church usually make up their minds from about 12 years onwards. **There is a special service for those who want to become adult members of the Church.**

The service is called confirmation. People agree to (ie confirm) the promises made for them at their baptism. Confirmation is so important that it is done by the bishop. He is a leader in the Church. He confirms people by placing his hands on their head.

Key words

confirmation
repent
grace

Before the bishop confirms people, he asks them questions such as these:

- Do you turn to Christ?
  I turn to Christ.
- Do you repent of your sins?
  I repent of my sins.
- Do you renounce evil?
  I renounce evil.

Candidates are also asked if they believe in God the Trinity:

- Do you believe and trust in God the Father?
- Do you believe and trust in his Son Jesus Christ?
- Do you believe and trust in the Holy Spirit?

Those being confirmed must understand what they are promising. They attend classes beforehand to learn more about their religion.

▲ *A bishop confirms a young woman*

23

▲ *The laying on of hands*

The bishop prays for those being confirmed. This prayer is from the Anglican service:

Defend, O Lord, these your servants with your heavenly grace,
that they may continue yours for ever, and daily increase in your Holy Spirit . . .

Caring touches and hugs are very important to people. They express love and acceptance. They make us feel safe and happy.

The moment of confirmation is when the bishop lays his hands on each person. He prays that the Holy Spirit will come to them. The bishop believes that he is passing on the power of the Holy Spirit handed down from person to person from the 12 disciples of Jesus. Like them, he is carrying on Jesus' work. It is as if Jesus himself is reaching down through the ages. To Christians, confirmation is a little touch of God.

Joy
Love
Peace
Kindness
Generosity
Patience
Faithfulness
Gentleness
Self-control

▲ *The fruits of the Spirit*

▲ *A hug shows someone cares when we need help*

Christians believe that the Holy Spirit will help them to become better people. The Bible lists 9 qualities that should grow in a person who claims to be a Christian. The Bible calls these the fruits of the Spirit.

This page is an example of the kind of thing young people are taught before they are confirmed.   It is about goodness and sin.

▲ *What would a Martian make of a piano?*

Imagine what would happen if an alien from Mars who couldn't hear was shown a piano. He would not know what to do with it.   He would not know what it is for.   He would probably use it wrongly.

In the same way, we are blind to the meaning of life.   We do not know what it is for.   We use our lives wrongly.

We need God to show us what to do with our life.   He gives our life a purpose.

Anything you do in line with what God wants for your life is good.   Anything which falls short of what God wants is called sin. The word 'sin' means 'to miss the mark'.

▼ *William Tell misses the mark*

1 Copy out and finish this paragraph:
Young people confirm their beliefs at a service called _____.   They agree to the _____ made by their _____ when they were babies.

2 Why does the cartoon show William Tell missing the mark?   What has this got to do with sin?   Explain as fully as you can.

3 Work with a small group.   Choose one of the fruits of the Spirit and work out a role-play to show someone with that quality in a particular situation.

Hands

4 Draw around your hands.   Write across them what the bishop's hands stand for in the confirmation service.   (Use ONE of the ideas on page 24.)

TASK: Talk about:
- Do you have something you believe in very strongly?
- How easy do you find it to share your beliefs with others?
- Do you mind if your friends have different ideas to you?

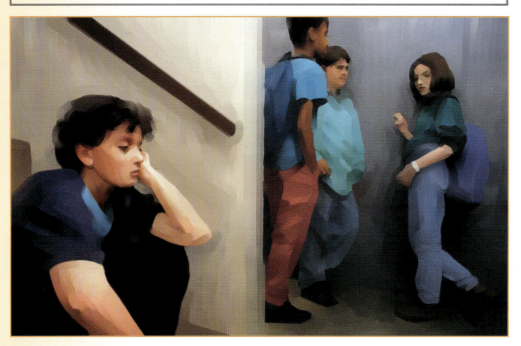

▲ *Some people always mock what they don't understand*

It is not always easy to be a Christian. Particularly if you are a teenager:

- Some people always mock what they don't understand. If a person has a strong faith, people sometimes make fun of them. They might shout 'alleluia' at them, or call them holy Joes. This can hurt. It makes people want to keep their religion to themselves.
- You might meet someone you really like and want to go out with. But that person has no time for your religion. You are young and want to have fun. But you want to be true to your beliefs, too.

Here some teenagers explain what being a Christian is like for them:

Marise (aged 19)
- At first my workmates were surprised I was in the Salvation Army. I looked too modern! But now they respect my beliefs. Sometimes people ask my opinion *because* I'm a Christian.

Mark (aged 16)
- Christians can feel at peace with anyone. They can love and forgive anyone if necessary. It is not easy, but it is a better way of living than if you're not a Christian.

Rosalind (aged 13)
- It helps me to feel that someone is always there to help me when I need it. It is important to me because Christianity is what I believe in.

Christian teenagers can get bored in church. The services might be old-fashioned and they may have nothing to do. Teenagers want to do things. They may want to worship in their own way, with lots of energy and fun. They want to worship with other young Christians.

There are many kinds of youth worship. One kind is like a Rave, with music and dancing, religious pictures, candles and incense.

Some teenagers like worship led by a modern band. They like to clap and raise their hands. Others prefer times of silence, with candle-light. They like to sit, kneel or lie on the floor.

Many church youth groups go away to special events like Greenbelt Arts Festival. This has modern bands of all styles. It has imaginative worship times. It has talks and Bible studie, and there is lots of fun.

◀ *Express yourself! A modern worship service gives people freedom to move around as they wish*

1 Using page 26, find THREE things that make it hard to be a Christian teenager.

2 Look back through the book so far and find FIVE things that Christians do which other people might find strange or difficult to understand. Why do people make fun of things they don't understand?

3 Read what Marise says on page 26.
a) Why were Marise's workmates surprised that she was in the Salvation Army?
b) What does that tell you about people's attitudes towards Christianity?

4 Using page 27, list FIVE things that make young Christians' worship more fun and exciting.

Key words

Salvation Army
incense

Prayer is talking and listening to God. Jesus asked his followers to pray on their own to God. Many Christians do this every day. Jesus said:

> Whenever you pray, go into your room and shut the door. Pray to your Father who is in secret. And your Father who sees in secret will reward you.
>
> *Matthew chapter 6 verse 6*

Prayers can be said sitting, standing, walking around, lying down or kneeling. There are no rules. Some people prefer to kneel because it shows that they feel small before God. Some make the sign of the cross on themselves.

Christians can make up their own prayers. Or they can read prayers from a book. They may say grace at meal-times, to thank God for the food.

Many people like to be still and silent in prayer:

> Be still and know that I am God.
>
> *Psalm 46 verse 10*

Here are 5 kinds of prayer:

1 Praise
Christians praise God for making the world. They want to tell him how great and good he is.

2 Thanks
Christians thank God for all the gifts he has given to the world, and for all that he has given them.

3 Asking forgiveness
Christians ask God to forgive their sins when they have done wrong.

4 Asking for yourself
They may be ill and ask God to make them better. They may ask for help in an exam.

5 Asking for others
Christians may ask God to make someone else better. Sometimes they may ask for something everyone wants, like world peace.

1 You have been asked to write the prayers for the Youth Service at a church. FIVE people will read the prayers. Write FIVE very short prayers – ONE for each different kind of prayer. Each prayer will start 'Dear God' and end 'Amen'.

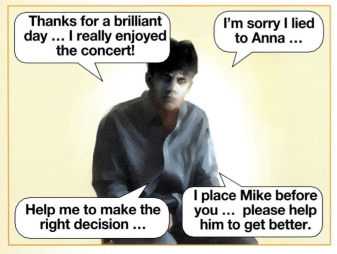

Thanks for a brilliant day … I really enjoyed the concert!

I'm sorry I lied to Anna …

Help me to make the right decision …

I place Mike before you … please help him to get better.

▲ *There are different kinds of prayer*

28

Does prayer work? What does it do? Here are some ideas:

It helps to think someone is listening.

Being quiet and asking for help often gives you the right idea.

There could be all kinds of links between our minds and other people's. Thinking good things might help good things to happen to them.

Prayer opens people up to God's power. It makes all kinds of things happen.

▲ *Christians have many ideas about prayer*

Christians do not expect prayer to work like magic, or a slot machine. They seek God's help and guidance. Sometimes people get what they pray for. Sometimes they don't. Sometimes a sick person is healed. Sometimes they are given inner strength and peace to cope with their illness.

All Christians use the Lord's Prayer. Jesus taught it to his followers:

Key words

praise
meditation

Our Father in heaven,
hallowed be your name,
your kingdom come,
your will be done,
on earth as in heaven.
Give us today our daily bread.
Forgive us our sins
as we forgive those who sin against us.
Lead us not into temptation
but deliver us from evil.
For the kingdom, the power, and the glory are yours
now and for ever.   Amen.

Sit still and comfortably in a quiet place.
Breathe deeply and slowly for a few minutes.
Imagine a peaceful scene.
Repeat a phrase over and over again, in your mind, such as 'May I be at peace ...'
Count 10 breaths and then open your eyes when you are ready to finish.

This kind of prayer is called meditation. It could be made into a Christian prayer by repeating Jesus' name or a verse from the Bible.

Some Christians like to do something when they pray, like lighting a candle. There are special candle-racks in some churches. Christians light a candle to show that they are offering prayers to God. The light stands for life and hope. Lighting candles is very popular today. People often light candles when someone has died.

▲ *Lighting a candle in prayer*

People take up different positions for prayer:
- Bowing shows respect to God.
- Kneeling shows that God is great.
- Open hands with arms raised show openness to God.
- Crossing yourself is a reminder of Jesus' death.
- Hugging yourself makes you feel safe in God's love.

▲ *People pray in different ways*

1 Read through the Lord's Prayer on page 29. How many of the different kinds of prayer on page 28 can you find in it?

2 Try the stilling exercise on page 29. How did it feel?

3 Ask your teacher to light a candle at the front of the class. All be very quiet and still. Each person adopts one of the positions of prayer shown on this page. Then each thinks in silence about someone they love, or somebody who is in great need, or something they care about a great deal. Afterwards, if you want to, talk about how you felt.

◀ *Drawing the sign of the fish*

When we talk about churches, most people think of church buildings. But a church is an assembly of Christians. They can meet anywhere. They don't really need special buildings, although there are now many kinds of church buildings.

In the years after Jesus died, Christians were forbidden to worship. So they met secretly to worship God. This was often in people's homes. Sometimes it was in underground tunnels where people were buried. These were called catacombs.

They had special signs to recognise each other. One was the fish sign. The word for fish in Greek was 'ichthus'. Each letter stood for a Greek word, meaning 'Jesus Christ, Son of God, Saviour'. You will still find this symbol being used by Christians today. There is also a new Church called Ichthus, with members in London and the south-east of England.

Another early Christian symbol was the chi-rho. This is made from the first 2 letters of the name 'Christ' in Greek.

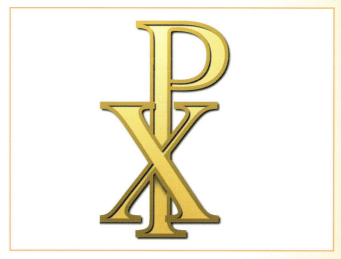

▲ *The chi-rho symbol*

1 Choose either the name Jesus or Christ. Make up a new Christian symbol from it.

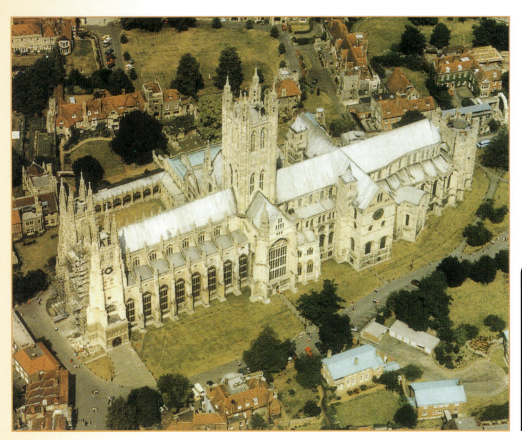

▲ *A view of Canterbury Cathedral from the air.   This is the church of the Archbishop of Canterbury.   He is the leader of the Anglican Church.   Notice that the building is in the shape of the cross*

Key words

catacombs
cathedral
chapel
Quakers
Mass
sermon

- Special, large churches where the bishop has his seat are called cathedrals.
- Small churches, attached to places like hospitals or schools, are called chapels.
- Quakers have meeting houses.
- The Salvation Army has citadels.

When you go into a church building, you will notice a main feature.   This tells you something important about that Church. For example:

- In a Roman Catholic church it is the altar. This tells us that Mass is the most important service in that Church.   That is because it takes place at the altar.
- In a Baptist church, the main feature is the pulpit.   This tells us that the Word of God is the most important part of the service. This is because the pulpit is used for preaching sermons on the Word of God.

▲ *Inside a Baptist church*

Inside an Anglican church.
Look for:

- the font where babies are baptised
- the altar, with a crucifix
- stalls where the choir sits
- kneelers, cushions to kneel on
- pews where people sit
- the pulpit for sermons
- the lectern for the Bible
- the hymn board

▲ *An Anglican church building with lots of interesting features*

1 a) What is the most beautiful building you have ever been in?

b) Why do you think church buildings are often very beautiful?

2 Look at the picture of the Anglican church above. What is its main feature?

3 Make a list of numbers 1–9. Against each number write the name of the item in the picture above.

4 You are an architect who has been asked to design a modern Christian place of worship. It must have places for people to sit. It must have an altar and a font, a lectern and a pulpit. Decide what shape it will be. Decide how it will be decorated. How will people know that it is a church? Write an explanation to explain why it is a good design.

◀ *Sharing a meal with friends*

TASK

Talk about:

- Which meals do you eat with other people?
- Which do you enjoy most? Explain why.

One person remembers this meal:

> We had been climbing in the Lake District, and we were very tired. We still had a long way to go, and everyone had finished their lunch ages ago. Then, someone pulled a pack of dried bananas out of their rucksack. They looked disgusting – all squashy, brown and wrinkly. But we didn't care, they were sweet and tasted good! We all gathered round and broke off bits and pieces so everyone had some. It gave us the energy, a lift, to keep going!

The last meal that Jesus ate with his disciples is called the Last Supper. He broke some bread and shared it with them, saying, 'Take, eat, this is my body.' Afterwards he passed round a cup of wine, saying, 'This is my blood which is shed for you. Do this in memory of me.'

▼ *Christians still share bread and wine.   Here are some of the names given to this special service:*

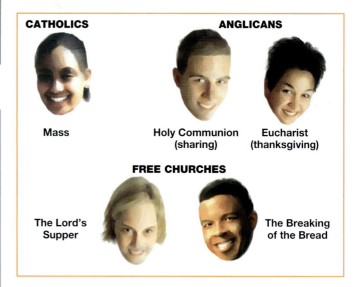

CATHOLICS — Mass

ANGLICANS — Holy Communion (sharing) / Eucharist (thanksgiving)

FREE CHURCHES — The Lord's Supper / The Breaking of the Bread

This is the most important service in many Churches. But Quakers and the Salvation Army do not have it. They say that God is with them in many ways, not just in bread and wine.

1 Write a menu for a special meal to share with friends.

Christians take Communion in different ways. The photos show 2 examples.

- In the Orthodox Church, the bread and wine are given together on a spoon. In other Churches they are given separately.
- Some Churches use flat, round wafers for the bread. They are specially made and have a cross stamped on them. Other Churches cut up ordinary bread into little pieces.
- Some Churches use wine, others have fruit juice.
- In some Churches, everyone drinks from a large goblet. In other Churches each person drinks from a small glass.
- In some Churches, the people come and kneel at the altar for Communion. In other Churches, it is brought round to them where they are sitting.

It is important for Christians to worship God together. Their main church service is on Sunday morning. This is the Christian holy day. It is the day of the week when Jesus is believed to have risen from death.

When Christians worship, they praise God for his greatness. They also say sorry for their sins. And they ask for guidance to live their lives better. There are different parts to a church service. It may include:

- prayers
- singing
- Bible readings
- sermon.

▼ *Orthodox Christians are given the bread and wine together from a spoon*

Christians worship God in different ways. When a priest came back to Wales from Jamaica, he noticed the difference:

A service at an African church in Kenya:

> We need more freedom in our worship. We should show love in our services and not just sit in our seats for 1 hour precisely. In Jamaica you put your watch away when you go to church. That was something I had to learn.
>
> They taught us to take time over worship and to sing more. Worship and church life is so important to Jamaicans. They all *belong* to a church. It is very important in their lives.
>
> *Network* magazine

> The people came singing, beating drums and dancing. When they reached the church, they all shouted 'alleluia' and came in. They carried on singing, jumping and making a lot of noise. When a church leader stood up, the singing stopped. There was a prayer which lasted 10 minutes. A man preached a sermon. Then 8 women stood up and confessed their sins. People gave money as they left the church. Some went home. The rest walked along the road, singing and praising the Lord.
>
> F B Welbourn and B A Ogot:
> *A Place to Feel at Home*

▲ *At this church in America, people clap and dance to the music, as well as sing*

Key words

Holy Communion
sermon

1 Design a poster to advertise a service of Holy Communion. Write on it the words of Jesus: 'This is my body' and 'This is my blood.'

2 List the different names for Holy Communion.

3 Ask your teacher to invite a Christian in to your class to talk about Holy Communion. Ask him or her to:
   a) describe how it is done at their church.
   b) explain why it is important for Christians, and what it means to them.

4 Match up the parts of the service (see page 35) with the correct furniture (see page 33):
prayers	pulpit
singing	lectern
Bible reading	choir stalls
sermon	kneelers

5 Read what the priest said about Jamaica. Work out from what he said what worship was like in his church in Wales.

One of the key people in a church is the person who leads the worship, the minister or priest. Churches have different names for this person, such as vicar or rector. They are all clergy. They use the title 'Reverend'. These people are trained over a number of years. They become clergy at a special service of ordination.

Some Churches have both men and women priests. The Roman Catholic Church has only men. Catholic priests are not allowed to get married. It is felt that a single man can give more time to his work.

So what do they do? We know that they take church services on Sundays, but what about the rest of the week? The pictures on page 38 show 2 days in the life of a vicar.

Not all clergy run churches. Some work as chaplains in schools or hospitals. This letter was sent to a hospital chaplain:

Dear Father John

Now that I'm home and getting over my operation, I'm writing to thank you for everything. You were a great help to me while I was in hospital.

I had never been in hospital before. It was all very strange for me. I felt alone and afraid as I waited for my operation. That was why it was so nice of you to spend time with me. Your kindness and sense of humour cheered me up. And the prayers you said for me made me feel calm and strong – especially when you put your hands on my head.

It was good of you to call to see me again after the operation and bring me Communion. I missed not being able to go to my own church ...

1 Talk about the advantages and disadvantages of priests being married. Record your points in 2 columns.

2 If you were in hospital, do you think you would like to be visited by a hospital chaplain? Talk about it with your partner.

chasuble · stole · surplice · alb · cassock

▲ *The priest on the left is dressed to take a Communion service. The priest on the right is dressed for the other morning and evening services*

Two days in a vicar's week

8:00: Went to church for silent prayer, then went home to do the washing-up.

9.00: Took assembly at the local church primary school.

9.30: Stayed in school and joined in a maths lesson with the children.

10.30: Spent break chatting to staff.

11.00: Christian Aid coffee morning at Mrs Brown's home.

12.00: Wrote an article for the parish magazine.

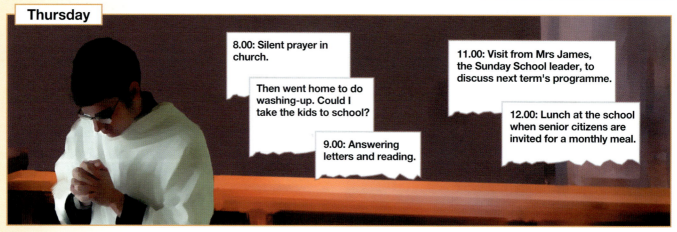

1.00: Lunch

2.00: Visited Miss Long who is 86 and housebound.

3.30: Saw Mrs Price. She visits newcomers to the congregation.

5.00: Evening Prayer. A chance to pray for people met during the day and to be quiet.

7.30: Played rounders with church youth group.

Thursday

8.00: Silent prayer in church.

Then went home to do washing-up. Could I take the kids to school?

9.00: Answering letters and reading.

11.00: Visit from Mrs James, the Sunday School leader, to discuss next term's programme.

12.00: Lunch at the school when senior citizens are invited for a monthly meal.

2.00: Visited sick parishioners in hospital and took Holy Communion to them.

4.15: Visited Mr Harvey whose wife died recently

5.00: Evening Prayer. Time for prayer and quiet. Then went home to be with the family.

7.00: Meeting with engaged couple to prepare them for their wedding in 6 weeks.

8.00-10.00: Adult Bible Study Group.

Ordained Women?

In Orthodox and Roman Catholic Churches the priests have to be men. The Anglican Church has recently allowed women to be priests. Most Protestant Churches have both men and women ministers.

Some of the arguments against having women priests are sexist:

- that a woman's place is in the home, and she wouldn't be able to run a family and a parish;
- that women would be too easily upset by some of the work;
- that women would find the job too tiring, since a priest is on call 24 hours a day.

But there is 1 argument that divides the Churches. At Holy Communion, the priest plays the part of Jesus Christ at the Last Supper. Many Christians think that the priest must be a man because Jesus was a man.

▲ *Dawn French as the TV Vicar of Dibley*

The Reverend Ros Parrett is a priest in Berkshire. She runs a church there. She speaks about being a woman priest:

> I was ordained priest in 1994. I worked at first in a team of priests. I have been the vicar of a town church since 1996.
>
> Yes, I have come across prejudice. But I have also had a great deal of support and prayer from all sorts of people.

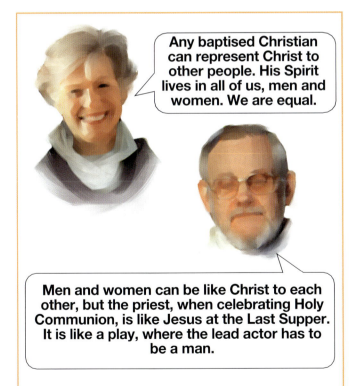

Any baptised Christian can represent Christ to other people. His Spirit lives in all of us, men and women. We are equal.

Men and women can be like Christ to each other, but the priest, when celebrating Holy Communion, is like Jesus at the Last Supper. It is like a play, where the lead actor has to be a man.

▲ *A woman and a man, both priests, have different views*

1 Ask your teacher to invite a local clergyman or clergywoman to talk to your class. Ask him or her:
   - why he or she became a priest
   - what his or her training involved
   - what happened at his or her ordination
   - what is the most important part of his or her work.

2 Look at the picture-strip on page 38.
   a) Make a note of the people he saw on their own.
   b) Think of ways the visits would have helped them. Talk about it with your partner.

3 Are there any parts of a Christian minister's work that you would like to do? Are there any parts you wouldn't like to do? Talk about this with a friend.

4 Write a letter to the *Church News* saying whether you agree/disagree with the ordination of women, explaining why.

◄ *People spend their leisure in all sort of ways. What do you spend most of your leisure time doing?*

TASK
- In pairs, talk about your favourite leisure activity.
- Work out how much leisure time you have a week.

Most people have a lot of free time. They have weekends, bank holidays and several weeks' holiday a year. School children have about three months' school holidays. People do lots of interesting things in their free time. The leisure industry is booming.

This was not always the case. Long ago, the only days off were holy days. This is where the word 'holiday' comes from. Even before Jesus' time, the Jews had a religious festival every Saturday – called the Sabbath.

After Jesus' death, Christianity spread beyond the Jews. **They chose Sunday as a new holy day because this was the day when Jesus rose from the dead.** They wanted to celebrate this.

At one time Christians were very strict about Sundays. There were all sorts of things they couldn't do on a Sunday. This idea came from the Jewish Sabbath, when no work is allowed.

300 years ago people were fined for selling things on a Sunday. Until recently, pubs had restricted opening hours, most shops were closed, and football matches were not played on Sundays. Now all this has changed.

Most Christians want Sundays to be special, but they don't want to lay down laws for other people who are not Christians. Most Christians like to relax, play sport and enjoy themselves on Sundays, as well as going to church.

But some Christians are still very strict about Sundays. They go to church for several hours, share meals together and relax. But they don't go shopping or do things which mean that other people have to work on Sundays.

I served in the Royal Air Force for 2 years and was sent off to the north of England. The first Sunday that I was allowed to leave camp I set off to find a church. I got back to camp late that night. Then the questions began.

Where had I been all day? 'I went to church.' That was clear enough, but where did I have my dinner? 'Oh, some people at the church took me home with them to dinner.' Did I know them before? 'No, I'd never set eyes on them before.' Well, what about tea? 'I had tea with another family.'

The other men were puzzled. They had not come across a family like that before – the family of the church.

Peter Cotterell: *This is Christianity*

▲ *Sunday Schools usually take place at the same time as the main church service. They are specially for the children. The children usually join the adults for part of the service*

We asked some Christians how they tried to make Sundays special. Here are 3 answers:

- **Sandy:** I always go to church on Sundays if I can, or attend the first Mass of Sunday held on Saturday evening. Sundays are my days off. No work or housework. It is a day to be with my husband. It is special because it is the only day when we can spend time together.

- **Lynne:** My mum has always gone to church and always took me along. So, Sunday has been the day when all other plans must fit around church ... For years, I have taught in Sunday School and, more recently, have also helped at a hospital chapel. So, in some ways, Sunday is also a day of service.

- **Alison:** We always go to church in the morning. We usually have a couple of the single young people from church to Sunday lunch. That's partly because when I was a young student in London, I used to go most Sundays to a family, and that meant so much to me.

Key word

Sunday School

1 What is the main thing that you would expect Christians to do on a Sunday? Explain why.

2 Sandy, Lynne and Alison all go to church on Sundays. Write down THREE more things that they do which make this day special for them.

3 You have been given an extra day off school. Plan what you will do and who you will spend it with.

TASK

In pairs, talk about whether or not you want to get married. Explain why or why not.

All Christian Churches have their own wedding services. They have their own customs, as you can see in the photo. But they all ask God to join the couple together and to make their marriage happy.

The vows are a very important part of a wedding service. These are the promises that the bride and groom make to each other. Imagine that Sarah and James are getting married in an Anglican church. They make the same vows:

The vicar would ask:

> James, will you take Sarah to be your wife? Will you love her, comfort her, honour and protect her, and, forsaking all others, be faithful to her as long as you both shall live?

James would say:

> I will.

▲ *The bride and groom make their vows to each other*

Soon afterwards, the vicar would place Sarah's right hand in James's right hand and James would repeat these words:

> I, James, take you, Sarah to be my wife, to have and to hold from this day forward; for better; for worse, for richer, for poorer, in sickness and in health, to love and to cherish, till death us do part, according to God's holy law; and this is my solemn vow.

The wedding ring is a symbol of the couple's love for each other. A circle has no end. In the same way, they hope that their love will go on forever.

Sadly, many marriages do not last forever. When a marriage breaks down, couples separate or divorce. The Christian Churches have different beliefs about this. These 2 are very different:

- The Roman Catholic Church does not accept divorce. They believe that if God joined the couple together, then people have no right to break it up. So if Catholics get divorced, they cannot have a church wedding if they want to marry again.
- The Orthodox Church allows divorce. They believe that even good marriages can go wrong. There are prayers of forgiveness when someone gets remarried.

Key words

vow
forgiveness

Here are some things that Christians say about marriage.

The Archbishop of Canterbury said:

> If we solved all our money problems and did not build loving families, it would not help us. The family is the place where the future is made good and full of love – or spoiled.

A Baptist said:

> In a marriage ceremony, you become one flesh, with God as head.   God is head of our marriage.   As we grow together, we should become closer to each other.   In so doing, we become closer to God.

A Catholic said:

> I would not have felt married in the eyes of the Church if I had been married elsewhere. My faith is important to me so I would not have felt happy within my marriage unless it had the blessing of the church.

Christians, for all their strong beliefs and hopes, might find that they fail each other. This is not always anyone's fault.   They may simply grow apart.   Or perhaps someone is at fault.   One partner may be cruel.   Or one partner may have an affair with someone else.   Whatever the cause, divorced people need love and support to build new lives.

▲ An Orthodox Christian wedding

1 Read the vows that are made in the first box on page 42.   List the FIVE promises.   In pairs, talk about their meaning.

2 Draw a wedding ring and write down its meaning.

3 Some people who get married in church hardly ever go to church.   What do you think about this?   Work out a role-play with a young couple and a Christian minister.   The couple do not attend church regularly but they want to get married there.   What reasons will they give for wanting to get married in church?

4 Look at what the Archbishop says about the family on this page.   Write your own views beginning 'The family is the place where ...' (Use about 50 words.)

5 Discuss:

a) Why does the Roman Catholic Church not accept divorce?

b) Do you think that divorced people should be allowed another church wedding? Explain your views.

The most important Christian festival is Easter. This is when Christians remember the death of Jesus and celebrate his Resurrection. The week before is called Holy Week. During Holy Week, Christians recall what happened in the last week of Jesus' life.

◀ *People welcome Jesus to Jerusalem*

Key words

Easter
Gethsemane
crucifix
Lent
Maundy Thursday

● The last week of Jesus' life

Palm Sunday
This was when people welcomed Jesus to Jerusalem. They waved palm branches. Jesus rode on a donkey because the Bible said, 'See, your king comes to you ... gentle and riding on a donkey.'

Monday – Wednesday
Jesus taught people in Jerusalem. But the Jews' leaders began to plot against him.

Maundy Thursday
This was the day of the Last Supper, when Jesus gave his disciples bread and wine (see page 34). He also washed his disciples' feet. This taught them to serve others, as Jesus was serving them.

▲ *Jesus washes the disciples' feet*

Later that evening, they went to the Garden of Gethsemane. Jesus knew that he was in danger. He prayed for a long time. Then soldiers came and arrested him. His disciples ran away.

Good Friday

▲ *Jesus is crucified*

Jesus was sentenced to death and hanged on a cross. The Romans thought that he was a troublemaker. Two thieves were crucified with him. One cursed him. The other asked for his help. Jesus said to him, 'Today, you will be with me in Paradise.' By the afternoon, Jesus was dead.

Holy Saturday

▲ *The garden tomb is closed with a heavy round stone*

Jesus was buried in a tomb cut into the rock. A huge stone was rolled across the entrance.

Easter Sunday

Early in the morning, some of the women followers of Jesus came to the tomb. They found the stone rolled back and the tomb empty. After that, his disciples saw Jesus both in Jerusalem and in Galilee.

▲ *The risen Christ appears to his disciples*

The disciples believed that Jesus was alive in a new way. After a while they did not see him any more. The disciples believed that he was taken up to heaven.

1 Draw a picture-strip for a child's comic of the events of the last week in Jesus' life.

2 Ask your teacher to show you a crucifix and a plain cross. The crucifix reminds Christians of Jesus' death. The plain cross reminds them of his Resurrection. Make up a new symbol for either his death or his Resurrection.

● Lent

Some Christians prepare for Easter for 40 days beforehand. This period is called Lent. It begins on Ash Wednesday. Some Christians have the sign of the cross made on their foreheads with ash. It is a sign of being sorry for their sins.

Christians make an extra effort in Lent. They may spend more time in prayer or helping others.

▼ *A Palm Sunday procession. Why do you think a donkey leads it?*

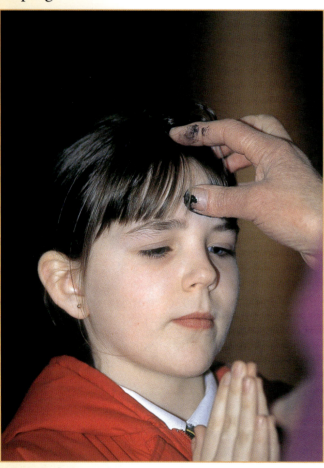

▲ *Ashes are used on Ash Wednesday*

● Holy Week

During this week, Christians recall what happened in the last week of Jesus' life.

Palm Sunday

Some Christians recall Jesus' entry into Jerusalem by carrying palm branches. Sometimes they have a donkey. They are given small crosses made from palm leaves.

Monday – Wednesday

They may have extra Communion services in the evening, or times of prayer.

Maundy Thursday

Christians remember the Last Supper. They call it 'Maundy' Thursday because 'maundy' means 'command'. After washing their feet, Jesus gave his disciples a new commandment. He said, 'Love one another, as I have loved you.' Many churches act out the washing of the feet. There is a special Holy Communion service on this evening which recalls the very first Communion given by Jesus.

Good Friday

▲ *Christians pay special respect to the cross*

On Good Friday, Christians remember the death of Jesus. Many churches remove all decorations so that they are plain and bare. The long story of Jesus' last week is read out from the Bible.

People may kiss a large crucifix. This is a cross with the figure of Jesus on it.

Why call this day *Good* Friday? Christians believe that Jesus had to die to save people. They say that he died instead of them, that he has paid for their sins.

Easter Eve

The first Easter service in some churches takes place after sunset on the evening of Holy Saturday. This celebrates the Resurrection. A fire is made outside the church and a very large candle is lit from it. This is called the Paschal candle. It is carried into the dark church, and everyone lights their own small candle from it.

▲ *Lighting the Paschal candle*

Easter Sunday

Joyful services celebrate the Resurrection. The church is full of flowers. Easter uses the theme of darkness and light. Jesus died but rose again. This teaches Christians that human life can be hard but that God will help them through it. Light follows darkness. Happiness follows tears.

1 Draw a picture-strip to show what Christians do each day of Holy Week up to Easter Day. This could be a group project.

2 Easter is about darkness turning to light. Make up a story where life is hard but it turns out alright in the end.

● Christmas

Easter is the most important Christian festival, but Christmas is the most popular. It celebrates the birth of Jesus Christ. The Bible does not say when Jesus was born. Christians picked 25 December because this was already a mid-winter festival.

Christians get ready for Christmas 4 Sundays beforehand. This period is called Advent. Many churches have an Advent ring of candles. This reminds Christians that the Bible calls Jesus the Light of the World.

▲ *An Advent ring. There is one candle to light each Sunday, and one in the middle for Christmas Day*

● Epiphany

Epiphany comes 12 days after Christmas on 6 January. This recalls the visit of the wise men from the East. It was the day when Jesus was 'shown' to the world. This is what 'epiphany' means. Eastern Orthodox Christians celebrate Christmas on this day.

Christians also remember the saints. December 6 is the saint's day of St Nicholas. He was a Turkish bishop in the 4th century. The legend of Santa Claus comes from him. One of his good deeds was that he threw 3 golden balls down a chimney. This was for 3 girls to get married and not be sold into slavery.

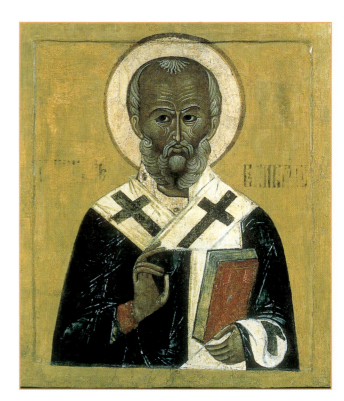

▲ *Icons are special pictures of the saints. They are painted with light around their heads (called a halo) and with light shining from their faces*

◀ *A dove and flames of fire represent the Holy Spirit*

Harvest

Churches hold Harvest festivals in the autumn. They thank God for nature and the food that is grown. People bring gifts of food to church to put on display. Afterwards it is given to old or poor people.

Sometimes money is collected for charities at the Harvest Thanksgiving service. It may be a charity like Christian Aid which feeds the hungry. Or it may be one to do with nature such as the charity called Trees for Life which plants new trees.

Pentecost

Another important festival is Pentecost. This recalls the gift of the Holy Spirit and the beginning of the Church. The story is told in the Bible where the symbols of wind and fire are used to describe the Holy Spirit. Like wind, God's Spirit cannot be seen, but people know he is there. Like fire, the Holy Spirit is warm and comforting, but also very powerful.

▲ *Some churches collect money for Trees for Life*

1 What events do Christians recall at:
   (a) Christmas   **(b)** Easter   **(c)** Pentecost?

2 Why is light used as a symbol at Advent and Christmas?

3 Why do you think saints are shown with light around their heads and with light shining from their faces?

4 Talk about the symbols of wind and fire:
   a) We can't see the wind, so how do we know if it is a windy day?
   b) In what ways is fire powerful?

5 In groups, make up your own festival to give thanks for trees. Where would it take place and what would happen?

Some Christians travel to a Christian centre to help them learn more about God.   This journey is called a pilgrimage.   People who make the journey are called pilgrims.

The places in this chapter are important pilgrimage centres.   You can see where they are on the map.

Key words

pilgrimage
pilgrim

▶ *This map shows some pilgrimage centres*

● Bethlehem

▲ *Inside the Church of the Nativity*

Bethlehem is in Israel.   A church was built where people think Jesus was born.   A star marks the spot.

● Jerusalem

Jerusalem is also in Israel.   It is where Jesus died.   Christians visit the Church of the Holy Sepulchre.   A sepulchre is a tomb. This church was built where people think Jesus was buried.

▲ *Inside the Church of the Holy Sepulchre*

● Rome

▲ *Pope John Paul II*

Rome is in Italy. It is where the Pope lives. He is the head of the Roman Catholic Church. Christians visit St Peter's Church. St Peter was one of the disciples. Catholics believe that he was the first Pope. He is thought to be buried under this church.

Christians go on pilgrimage:

- to see important Christian places
- to try to get healing
- to get closer to God
- to get away from the world for a while.

● Lourdes

▲ *Lourdes*

Lourdes is in France. This town became famous about 150 years ago. A poor girl named Bernadette had visions of Mary the mother of Jesus. Mary told her where to dig for a spring of water. Christians visit the spring and the church that was built there. Some people have been healed there.

1 Match up these places and descriptions:

Bethlehem   where the Pope lives
Jerusalem   where Bernadette saw Mary
Rome   where Jesus died
Lourdes   where Jesus was born

2 In groups of 4, each select a different reason for going on pilgrimage. Invent a personal story for your reason. Act out a scene where you meet on pilgrimage and share your stories.

There are important places of pilgrimage in Britain too.

Canterbury

▲ *The Archbishop of Canterbury, George Carey (centre), with visitors*

Canterbury is in Kent. This is where Christianity first came to England. The Archbishop of Canterbury lives here. He is the most important bishop in the Church of England. His church is Canterbury Cathedral. Nearly 1000 years ago, an Archbishop of Canterbury was murdered in the cathedral. His name was Thomas a Becket. Christians visit the place where he was killed.

Walsingham

Walsingham is in Norfolk. Like Lourdes, it is famous because people believe that Mary appeared there. This happened about a 1000 years ago. Mary told a rich lady to build a copy of the house where Jesus grew up in Nazareth. Again, a spring of water appeared. Pilgrims came from all over Europe to drink the water and pray. There were stories of miracles.

In the 16th century the building was destroyed by Henry VIII. He wanted its riches. It lay in ruins until nearly 100 years ago. Then money was raised to rebuild it. Today there is a new shrine Church with a new Holy House inside. People still come here and drink the water. They come for healing and peace.

Key word
shrine

▶ *Inside the Anglican shrine of Our Lady of Walsingham*

52

● Miracles on pilgrimage

Many people say they have been healed at places like Lourdes and Walsingham. If you went there you would see many photos and letters of thanks, like the before-and-after photos below. This woman was ill for 13 years before bathing in the waters at Lourdes. The Catholic Church accepted this as a miracle. They ask these questions:

- Was the illness serious?
- Was the cure sudden?
- Was it a complete cure?
- Did it last for at least 3 years?
- Was it proved by tests, X-rays, etc?
- Did any medical treatment help the cure?

Before

After

▲ *Edeltraud Fulda before and after her miracle cure*

Andrea's story

Andrea Jackson had a serious accident when she was 8. Her parents spoke about it on a TV programme about Walsingham:

> They told us that Andrea wasn't expected to live the night. Surgeons had removed a large part of her skull. We were prepared for the worst.
>
> She was unconscious for most of a week. We had decided that we wouldn't allow her to be kept alive on a machine.

> Then another girl was anointed at the Holy Well in Walsingham instead of Andrea. And at the same time holy water was sprinkled on Andrea in hospital. They brought her round and took the tubes out of her nose and throat. She looked around and said, 'I've been to Walsingham.' We stood back in amazement. We couldn't understand why she said that.
>
> BBC Television: *England's Nazareth*

▼ *Andrea's parents believe that she was healed at Walsingham*

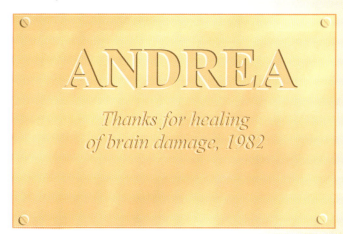

ANDREA

Thanks for healing of brain damage, 1982

1 Talk about these questions in groups:
   a) Do you believe in miracles?
   b) Have you ever heard of someone who has been healed by a miracle?

2 Talk about this in pairs:
   a) Do you think Andrea's cure was a miracle? Give your reasons.
   b) What did you find most surprising about Andrea's story?

3 You are the leader of a group of Christians going on pilgrimage. Choose where you are going and design a banner to carry with you. Explain why you chose your design.

The *Star Trek* series has a mission for its crew: 'to boldly go where no man has gone before' in the universe. A mission is a task that you are sent on. It doesn't have to be religious.

Jesus sent his followers on a mission. Their task was to carry on his work. They were to teach people about God. They were to show God's love in action.

A Christian missionary is someone who goes somewhere to work for Jesus. A missionary can be a man or woman, a priest, monk or nun, or an ordinary Christian.

Here is an advert for missionaries:

▲ *Protestors with a mission. These people from Greenpeace are protesting against nuclear power*

YES!
missionaries still exist.
NO!
missionaries are not out of date.

Missionaries? Missions? The name doesn't matter, but . . .

Middle East Christian Outreach

is glad to be a fellowship of those who believe in reaching out in the love of Jesus Christ to lost men and women.

Middle East Christian Outreach

needs missionaries - or whatever you like to call people who are willing to move with God, wherever, however and whenever he directs.

WHAT KIND OF PEOPLE ARE NEEDED?

▲ *Part of a pamphlet from Middle East Christian Outreach (MECO)*

MISSIONARY JOBS

RUN SCHOOLS
RUN HOSPITALS
RUN MEDICAL CENTRE
TRAIN OTHERS TO TAKE OVER
HELP DURING FAMINE
PREACH
CONVERT

▲ *Missionary work*

Missionaries today don't only tell people about Jesus. They also put Christian love into action. Some are teachers, for example. Some are doctors and nurses. Some are engineers.

This bishop was a missionary in the Sudan:

> I was asked by some local schoolboys why I had come to the Sudan. I could only say something like this, '... because I believe somehow that God has called me. Don't ask me to explain how. ... And because it offered adventure in the service of Jesus Christ.'

Key words

mission
missionary

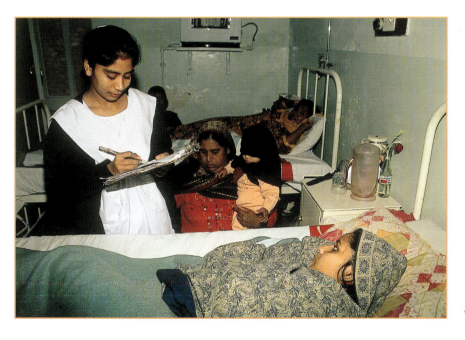

◀ *Some missionaries work in hospitals*

1 In pairs, look at the list of missionary jobs above. Which TWO do you think are most important for Christian mission? Explain why.

2 Talk with a partner about each of these qualities, explaining why it is important for missionaries to have them:
- cheerful and not depressed by problems
- hard-working and full of energy
- brave
- kind and caring towards others
- doesn't often get ill
- has a skill, such as a teacher, doctor or engineer
- a strong Christian.

3 In groups, think up a worthwhile mission for today's world (eg saving the rainforests). Think about the skills that would be needed. Write an advert, asking for people with certain skills to help with this mission.

Some Christian men and women become monks and nuns. They make 3 promises so that they can give themselves totally to God's work:

Never to get married	Not to own money	To obey their own rules

▲ *The 3 promises*

Years ago monks and nuns wore simple robes like poor people. Today, these robes make them look different from everyone else. Many have now started to wear modern clothes. These are often more practical for their work. Some monks and nuns keep to themselves and pray. They work with their hands and on their land. Others go out and help people.

▲ *Nuns running a 'soup kitchen'*

One group of nuns lives at St Saviour's Priory in the East End of London. The nuns wear modern dress. They work among the local housing estates. Some help in local primary schools. Some run drop-in centres. Some visit the sick and elderly. Some are there to listen to people's worries. Some give meals and hot drinks to the homeless.

They also help people to make a retreat. A retreat means spending a few days away from your job. It is a time of quiet and prayer. Also, people often ask the nuns to pray for them.

▲ *This monk wears robes. He has a belt with 3 knots in it for the 3 promises*

▲ *Mother Teresa*

Mother Teresa is the most famous nun of modern times.   She died in 1997.   She set up the Sisters of Charity.   They opened their first Home for the Dying in 1952 in Calcutta, India.   These sisters (nuns) took in people they found dying on the streets. Often they were old people, but sometimes they were just babies.   Mother Teresa wanted to show these people the love of Christ, even in the last days of their life.

She said:

- Being unwanted is the worst disease of all. Nowadays there are cures for all kinds of diseases.   But being unwanted will never be cured unless there are willing hands to serve and a loving heart to love.

- Every person is Christ for me.   Since there is only one Jesus, that person is the only person in the world for me at that moment.

1 a) Draw a rope down your page, about 10 lines long.   Draw THREE knots in the rope. Write against them the 3 promises made by monks and nuns.

b) Have you ever made an important promise?   If so, was it difficult to keep?

2 a) What does it mean to go on retreat?
b) Have you ever wanted to get away from it all?   What did you do about it?

3 Put the title 'Nun's work' in the middle of a page or piece of paper.   Use it as the centre of a spidergram.   List around it at least TEN different things nuns do.   Use pages 56–57 to find the answers.

Soap operas are popular. We follow the stories and get hooked. In a way, they are about real life. But they are also larger than life. They involve:

- relationship problems
- family break-ups and get-togethers
- sudden tragedies (illness, car-crash, etc).

People in soaps usually want their own way. If other people get hurt, then that's sad, but it's life. Theirs is a very modern message: 'Put yourself first.'

▲ *Should a Christian give away everything to the poor?*

People sometimes think that Christians should be the complete opposite of this. They think they should always put others first. They think they should give away all their money to charities. They think they should do everything for love. (Priests are often asked by young people, 'Do you get paid?')

There are some parts of the Bible which may lead people to think this way. But Jesus also said, 'Love your neighbour as yourself.' This gets things into balance. Christians must love themselves as well as other people. In fact, if you can't love yourself, you are not much good to anyone else.

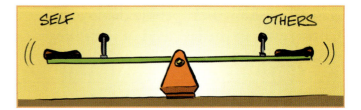

There are no easy answers for a Christian lifestyle. Each Christian must find their own balance between making choices for themselves and for others. They will get help in this by talking things through at church, and by praying about it.

58

● Sex

Trust is very important in a close friendship. When you get close to someone, you open up to them. You stop putting on an act. You are just yourself. You let your friend see your weaknesses. Relationships break down when that trust is broken.

> **TASK**
>
> In small groups, think of ways in which trust can be broken in a relationship (eg by making fun of your friend behind his or her back).

There are even deeper feelings in a sexual relationship. The couple share at a deeper level. The Bible writers spoke of having sex as 'knowing' someone. This is what Christians think sex should be. It shouldn't be taken lightly. The Church teaches that when people have sex too freely, it loses its true meaning.

> **TASK**
>
> In small groups, talk about the risks of having sex too freely. Think about people's feelings as well as other risks.

The Church has laid down rules about sex. This is because it is so precious and it can be spoilt so easily. The Church has taught that sex should only take place within marriage.

But what about couples who live together before marriage? They have made a commitment to each other. They are faithful to each other. They will probably get married after a few years. The Church has not changed its teaching about this. But some clergy say that the commitment to another person is the important thing.

'If you love me you will ...'

▲ *Sometimes one partner puts pressure on the other to have sex*

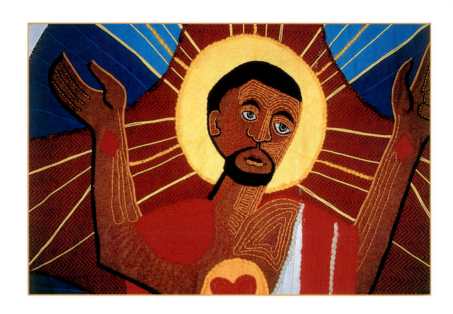

▶ *Jesus is shown here with black hair and dark skin*

● Racism

Soap operas often deal with racism. Racism is when people are treated differently just because of their race or colour. There are many causes of racism:

- fear of people who are different
- fear of people from other countries taking all the jobs
- feeling that our ways are better than theirs
- ignorance about other people.

A white couple were racist about Asians. It so happened that their son's best friend was an Asian. But he kept it a secret from his parents. When he finally brought his friend home, his parents were fine with him. Afterwards their son said, 'Why were you so kind to him? You said you didn't like Asians.' His parents said, '*He* was alright – it's all the others we don't like.' This story shows that people often fear and dislike what they do not know or understand. When you get to know someone, you quickly forget the colour of their skin.

Christianity teaches that there is one God and all people are his children. All are equal before God. There are Christians all over the world, of every race and colour. Jesus himself came from the Middle East. He would have had dark hair and skin.

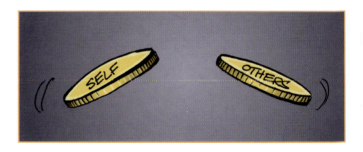

1 On page 58 a see-saw showed the importance of balancing self and others. The same thing can be shown by 2 sides of a coin. Think of another way to show this balance. Draw it and write underneath the words of Jesus: 'Love your neighbour as yourself.'

2 You have been asked to produce a leaflet called 'Beware of Racism' for a church youth group. Design the cover, and inside explain the Christian teaching against racism.

> ● I will show you my faith by my actions.
> *James chapter 2 verse 18*
>
> ● I give you a new commandment that you love one another.
> *Jesus, in John chapter 13 verse 24*

The world changes all the time, and there are new problems to face. Christians do not think that they have all the answers. After all, Jesus did not teach about AIDS, drugs or nuclear war. Many modern problems did not exist then.

But **Christians try to show the love that Jesus showed, whatever the problem. Jesus accepted people who were turned away by others. Christians try to do the same today.**

▲ *A lesson on the dangers of drugs – a problem which did not exist when Jesus was alive*

In this chapter we look at 2 different Christian groups. We see what they are doing to follow Jesus today.

● The Salvation Army

This is actually a Church, but it is best known for its social work. This is what it has to say about itself:

> Members of the Army are called Salvationists. They are involved in many kinds of activities:
> ● preaching the gospel
> ● running playgroups
> ● playing in bands
> ● treating sickness
> ● praising God
> ● praying
> ● studying the Bible
> ● feeding the hungry
> ● caring for the homeless
> All of these activities have the same purpose – to make the world a happy place, for God's sake.

And here, a member of the Salvation Army describes a typical night's work:

> It is nearly midnight. The little blue van heads towards fashionable Oxford Street. There is nobody to be seen. Suddenly the piles of cardboard by the wall begin to move. Men are sleeping under the cardboard boxes.
> Soon 20 men are waiting for supper. Everybody knows the Captain and his team. There is no preaching. The men are warmed and cheered as they drink the soup and eat the bread.
> An observer said it was like Jesus giving out the bread and wine.

Christian Aid

We believe in life before death

Christian organisations also work to try to improve conditions in countries other than Britain. One such organisation is Christian Aid

● Christian Aid

Christian Aid helps people in poor countries. It gives emergency help when disasters strike. It also helps people to help themselves.

▲ *These girls are being vaccinated to stop the spread of disease*

▲ *Friada cuts her crops with a shell*

1 a) Work in small groups. Each group is to write a letter either to the Salvation Army or to Christian Aid, asking for more information about what they do. (Their addresses are: The Salvation Army, 101 Queen Victoria Street, London EC4P 4EP; Christian Aid, PO Box 100, London SE1 7RT.)
b) With the material, make a wall display to show how Christians are making the world a better place.
2 Talk about:
a) What other problems face the world today?
b) Do you know of any organisations which are trying to deal with these problems?
c) How could you help?

Friada works in rice fields in Africa. She has to cut the crops with a large snail shell because she has nothing else to use. Imagine how long it takes! The nearest market is 15 miles away, and the roads are poor. Christian Aid provides a tractor to carry the heavy crops to market.

Christian Aid gives money to schools in Haiti. It is for vaccinations to help stop disease.

Advent – the Church's time of preparation before Christmas

Anglican – of the Church of England

Apocrypha – books accepted as part of the Bible by Catholics but not Protestants

Ascension – when Jesus went up to heaven

baptism – dipping in water to make someone a member of the Church

Bible – Christian holy book

catacomb – underground burial place

cathedral – church building where there is a bishop

chapel – a place where Christians worship

Christmas – festival to celebrate the birth of Jesus Christ

confirmation – ceremony to become an adult member of the Church

conscience – inner voice, sense of right and wrong

creed – list of beliefs

cremate – to burn up a dead body

crucifix – cross with figure of Jesus on it

crucifixion – death on a cross

curate – assistant priest

disciples – followers of Jesus

Easter – festival to celebrate the death and resurrection of Jesus Christ

Eastern Orthodox – Churches of Eastern Europe

Epiphany – festival to recall the visit of the wise men to the child Jesus

font – basin holding water for baptism

forgiveness – wrong-doings are set aside

funeral – service for someone who has died

Gethsemane – the Garden of Gethsemane where Jesus was arrested

Good Friday – the day when Jesus died

Gospel – 'good news' about Jesus, book of what Jesus said and did

Grace – unearned favour

heaven – where people are rewarded after death

Holy Communion – Christian ceremony to share bread and wine

Holy Spirit – the Spirit of God

hymn – religious song in verses

incense – spice which gives off a sweet smell when burned

inspire – to put thoughts in your mind

Jesus Christ – the key figure in Christianity

Lent – 40 days to prepare for Easter

Mass – Roman Catholic name for Holy Communion

Maundy Thursday – the day of the Last Supper

meditation – silent, thoughtful prayer

miracle – amazing event which goes against the laws of nature

mission – a task you are sent to do

missionary – person who travels to spread Christianity

mystery – something that can't be explained

New Testament – part of the Bible which tells the Christian story

obituary – a statement written about a person after their death

Old Testament – first and oldest part of the Bible

Orthodox (see Eastern Orthodox)

pilgrim – someone who goes on a religious journey

pilgrimage – a religious journey to a holy place

Pope – leader of the Roman Catholic Church

praise – joyful worship of God

priest – an ordained minister of the Church

Protestant – those who protested against the Catholic Church, and broke away

Quaker – a Christian Church, also called the Society of Friends

repent – to be sorry

Resurrection – coming back to life

Roman Catholic – Church in the West, led by the Pope

Salvation Army – a Christian Church

sermon – a religious talk given in a service

shrine – holy place

sin – wrong-doing, against God's will

Sunday School – children's meeting at church

symbol – something that stands for something else

Trinity – 3-in-1 God

vow – promise

Index